'Brexit has put in question much of the traditional fabric of the constitution. *Unwritten Rule* is a brave attempt to show how it can be remoulded. While few will agree with all of the proposed remedies, *Unwritten Rule* will undoubtedly reinvigorate the debate. It is written with clarity and verve by experienced practitioners in government.'

— Vernon Bogdanor, Professor of Government, King's College London

'A timely, compelling, and extremely important contribution to the most pressing political debate of the next decade. Can we reinvent the UK for the next century as it has so often been reinvented in the past? The authors suggest a series of positive steps, including constitutional reform and significant devolution in England, in the hope that the nations and regions of the UK can find enough common ground to prevent a painful dissolution of the Union.'

— Gavin Esler, author of *How Britain Ends: English Nationalism and the Rebirth of Four Nations*

HAUS CURIOSITIES

Unwritten Rule

About the Contributors

Stephen Green was Chair of HSBC between 2006 and 2010 and later Minister of State for Trade and Investment. He has been a member of the House of Lords since 2010.

Thomas Legg served as a career civil servant in the Lord Chancellor's Department (now the Ministry of Justice) and as its Permanent Secretary under three prime ministers from 1989 to 1998.

Martin Donnelly was Permanent Secretary of the Departments of Business and then International Trade from 2010 to 2017. He has worked in a range of central government departments including the Cabinet Office, Foreign Office, and Treasury.

Stephen Green, Thomas Legg, Martin Donnelly

UNWRITTEN RULE

How to Fix the British Constitution

First published by Haus Publishing in 2021
4 Cinnamon Row
London SW11 3TW
www.hauspublishing.com

A CIP catalogue record for this book is
available from the British Library

Print ISBN: 978-1-913368-30-2
Ebook ISBN: 978-1-913368-31-9

Typeset in Garamond by MacGuru Ltd

Printed in Czech Republic

Contents

Preface

The United Kingdom faces a constitutional crisis that could lead to its break-up within the next few years. It is becoming clear that there are now fundamental challenges to its political cohesion and underlying constitutional structure. These challenges have become more urgent and complex over the last decade, with the consequences of the Scottish independence referendum in 2014 and the Brexit referendum in 2016 continuing to be felt. Maintaining the consent of all parts of the nation for a United Kingdom that is relevant to a new generation of voters will depend on whether we can offer a more appealing vision of that Union. The Union needs to be more inclusive, varied, and open if it is to remain a meaningful part of our identity and if the state is to serve its people effectively. We offer the proposals in this book as one contribution to the wider, urgent debate about the scale and focus of this necessary change.

We have based this short book on ideas we first set out in a paper on constitutional reform for the Policy Reform Group in January 2021. Our thanks go to John

Llewellyn, Chair of the Policy Reform Group, for his support and encouragement, as well as to Andrew Gowers for his editorial support and critical comments as we were bringing our thoughts together for that paper.

Introduction: The Emerging Crisis of Governance

On 1 January 2021, the British state began a new chapter in its history. More than a decade of struggle over the future of its relationship with the European Union finally came to a point of closure. Legally, the United Kingdom had already left the EU, but negotiations over a new set of agreements with Brussels had been fractious. They were finalised almost at the last minute, and the new deal was approved by parliament just in time for it to come into force at the start of the new year. The government claimed it had 'got Brexit done' and that a new era of sovereign liberty had begun.

But this new chapter does not look to be a story of calm after the storm. In the midst of the pandemic, the government had moved very close to the cliff edge of a rancorous no-deal exit. The storm may be abating, and we may have stepped back from the edge, but now the government finds itself uncomfortably close to another abyss: the possible break-up of the United Kingdom.

Confidence in the integrity of the British state is at its

lowest level since the Republic of Ireland became independent 100 years ago. The Brexit process has exposed the deepening divisions between the nations of the UK. Northern Ireland now operates under trading rules that are legally separate from the rest of the UK, and it may be drawn increasingly towards the EU through its open border with the Republic. Meanwhile, even in Wales – where nationalism has always been more cultural than political – opinion polls show that support for independence is running at a historical high of about 25 per cent.[1] But above all, Scotland is more conscious than ever of its separate identity and its aspirations for a European future, and opinion polls are now consistently indicating a clear majority for independence. Negotiations between the UK government in Westminster and the Scottish National Party-led government in Holyrood over a referendum will be politically tense. And if a referendum results in a vote for independence, the consequent negotiations over the terms will be at least as complex as – and even more emotionally charged than – the last five years of wrangling with Brussels.

Meanwhile, the 'English problem' remains largely unresolved. England itself is too big in relation to the rest of the UK for it to be devolved as a single entity, but its regional identities are relatively weak compared with the clear national identities of Scotland and

Wales. Devolution within England has therefore proceeded on a somewhat ad hoc basis, with no systematic strategy for devolving power and responsibility to its cities or regions. Moreover, the early stages of the coronavirus pandemic exposed some of the weaknesses of a highly centralised English administration that concedes less fiscal and regulatory power to regions and local authorities than any other comparable democratic system. As a consequence, we have seen the growing assertiveness of some metropolitan mayors (particularly those of Manchester and London) in challenging the Westminster government to make an effective reality of devolution.

At the same time, public trust and confidence in government has in recent years fallen to record lows, while interest in politics (primarily driven by the passionate debates over Brexit) is at its highest for at least the last twenty-five years, according to a British Social Attitudes survey.[2] Few outside the world of Westminster now believe that parliament is an effective forum for discussing and determining national priorities. The overly adversarial nature and behaviour of the Commons is widely perceived as unhelpful and unedifying. And virtually all agree that the House of Lords is in need of significant reform, even though there is no consensus on how this should be done.

Moreover, recent moves by the government – including both the illegal prorogation of parliament in 2019 and the proposal (in the Internal Market Bill, which came before parliament in the autumn of 2020) to give ministers the authority to override international treaty obligations – have called into question the stability of British institutions and the values that underpin them. The offending clause in the Internal Market Bill was later dropped in the face of cross-party resistance, particularly in the House of Lords – but not before Britain's sovereign rating was downgraded by Moody's, the highly influential credit rating agency, to a level below that of France for the first time in many years. In their report, Moody's referred explicitly to 'weakened institutional policy effectiveness' and to an erosion in 'respect for rules and norms'.[3]

All in all, the UK faces the most pressing need since the formation of the Irish Free State 100 years ago to review its governance and ensure its viability and integrity as a state. Reform is needed both to improve the effectiveness of government and also to offer a compelling case for the Union, whose very existence is now under challenge from Scotland.

Part 1: The Need for Radical Reform

The governance of the UK will always have its own distinctive form, shaped by the history of the country. But the assumption that what has worked will continue to work is increasingly dangerous. We believe that now is the time for a clear and honest look in the mirror; and we also believe that there are particular characteristics of a number of comparator democracies which will be relevant as we review the major constitutional issues now facing the UK.

Parliament: the need to adjust to an emerging, more federal settlement

Until the turn of this century, the UK was effectively a unitary state (except for the special circumstances of Northern Ireland) in which all significant political life was centred at Westminster. The national legislatures of Scotland and Wales are only just over twenty years old.

Since then, however, the devolved administrations have gained in power and influence. The three devolved parliamentary institutions now command substantial public support and are responsible for a wide range of social and economic activities. Essentially, the reserved powers of the UK government relate mainly to finance and macroeconomics, defence and security, border control and immigration, and international relations. As a result, an increasing proportion of legislation coming before the Westminster parliament applies only to England, since there is no separate parliament of England. This consequence has been recognised since 2016 by procedures at Westminster that allow only MPs representing English constituencies to vote on legislation that applies only to England.

There are two fundamental problems with this status quo. First, the devolution settlement of 1997 is contested and unstable, seen as based on a set of short-term political compromises rather than clearly understood and agreed principles. Second, devolution within England is at best a work in progress, with the balance between the centre and regions more weighted to the centre than is the case in any other major comparator polity.

For the UK as a whole, the devolution settlement is fraying, especially in Scotland. With the SNP's rise to power and in the wake of the Brexit vote, the momentum for Scottish independence may now be unstoppable. In the process of leaving the EU, the UK government used Brexit to reassert its control over a range of economic activities that had previously been subject to the rules of the EU Single Market or other EU frameworks – from trading to fishing and financial services. In doing so, the devolved governments argued, it was flying in the face of the Sewel Convention – agreed in 1999 by the UK government at that time – which states that the UK parliament will 'not normally' legislate without the consent of the devolved legislatures in cases where the proposed legislation impacts their powers. The Supreme Court ruled in 2017 that the Sewel Convention remains a purely political convention, which is not justiciable. The EU Withdrawal Act and the UK Internal Market Act were thus passed despite their impact on devolved powers and against the strong opposition of the three devolved governments.

Against this background of exacerbated tension between Westminster and the devolved legislatures, the fact that majorities in both Scotland and Northern Ireland voted in the 2016 referendum to remain in the EU has created entirely new complexities. In the case of Scotland, it has created a new momentum for independence that may be impossible to reverse without radical change. It is also possible that, over time, this could lead to agreed changes in the relationship between Northern Ireland and the Republic, an outcome explicitly allowed for in the Good Friday/Belfast Agreement. As a result, the working-out of the new relationship between the UK and the EU could accelerate the eventual, consensual integration of Northern Ireland into the Republic of Ireland. Constitutionally, such an outcome in Northern Ireland would simplify the UK's position (and it would also simplify the UK's ongoing relationship with the EU, because the Belfast Agreement and the Northern Ireland Protocol would no longer be needed).

For Scotland, however, a new referendum resulting in a majority for independence would trigger complex negotiations involving the break-up of an integrated polity that is almost 300 years old. The whole process would be at least as difficult and protracted as the Brexit negotiations with the EU. It would also pose serious risks for both Scotland and the remaining UK.

The SNP has made clear its objective to achieve full sovereignty. Were Scotland then to become an EU member state – also a clear goal of the SNP – the UK's ongoing relationship with Scotland would effectively mirror its relationship with the Republic of Ireland. The transition would create unique issues of defence, security, and foreign policy for the UK, as well as all the pressing questions about trade and investment experienced on the island of Ireland following Brexit. The Irish precedent of unrestricted movement between the countries would presumably be followed, and a new Scottish government would have to decide on highly sensitive questions about national identity qualifications, such as who would have the right to Scottish citizenship (which would give EU residency rights) – an issue likely to be of interest to many millions residing in England with close Scottish family connections.

But this is not just a Scottish crisis. The decision on Scottish independence will certainly also have reverberations in both England and Wales. The demand in Wales for effective home rule will become ever more insistent. And the 'English question', already posed starkly by the divisive experience of the pandemic, will be thrust further into the spotlight. Devolution has, in recent decades, led to substantial decentralisation of executive and operational functions for Scotland, Wales, and Northern Ireland. But England remains the most centralised large polity in the whole of the Western democratic world.

Even France – probably, of all our natural comparators, the most like England in its tradition of centralisation – now has strong mayoralties and regional councils. France has gone from Napoleonic centralisation, with *préfets* and *sous-préfets* acting as the executive agents of Paris across France, to a much more decentralised system where communes, municipalities, and regions all work together with significant autonomy. England, by contrast, used to be more decentralised than France, with county councils having real financial and executive powers. The two systems changed places in the 1980s, when France decentralised under President Mitterrand and the UK removed fiscal power from local authorities through rate capping and hypothecated grants.

There are, however, serious obstacles to reform. England has been a relatively centralised country since the Norman Conquest in 1066. English governments have always tended to think in centralised terms and have been reluctant to cede real autonomy to regional centres of power. This tendency is part cause and part consequence of relatively weak regional identities, at least in political terms. The only regional polities England has ever had – the ancient kingdoms of Mercia, Northumbria, Wessex etc. – have no continuing relevance even as folk memories, and county loyalties surface mainly in cricket. The only serious attempt since the Second World War to create regional democratic institutions in England – that of the Blair government in the early years of the new millennium – came to an embarrassing halt when the people of the north-east voted overwhelmingly (on a low turnout) against the establishment of a regional assembly in 2004.

Since then, decentralised democratic representation has evolved in a different direction. Over twenty cities and metropolitan areas now have directly elected mayors (some of whom have established national reputations). This is a significant development, driven increasingly firmly by central government ever since the coalition of 2010 to 2015. Yet the powers of these elected mayoralties remain limited, particularly in regard to funding. True federalism implies giving these units significant authority to make their own decisions about how and at what level public services are provided. To do so would require meaningful power to raise and allocate funding, without which electoral accountability becomes one-sided and weak (with elected mayors too easily able to blame central government for their failure to deliver on electoral promises). Such financial powers would in turn require a radical change in the traditional Treasury orthodoxy, which has always sought to avoid or minimise any decentralisation or hypothecation of tax-raising other than in very special circumstances, such as those that led to the Barnett formula (dating from the 1970s), which automatically adjusts central government spending allocated to the devolved nations.[4]

All this pressure for devolution has profound implications for the Westminster parliament. Despite the imperfections of the status quo – and notwithstanding occasional outbursts of irritation by central government at the complexities it involves – devolution seems to be a one-way street. The centralising instincts of both Westminster and Whitehall have not entirely faded; indeed, theoretically, all the devolved powers discussed above could be revoked by a single act of the Westminster parliament. Yet this would be plainly impossible, given the political realities of the modern era. Devolution therefore necessarily raises fundamental questions about the role and authority of the Westminster parliament. Furthermore, the competence and efficiency of Westminster have increasingly come under the spotlight in recent decades. The need for reform is contested and contentious in the case of the Commons, but it is universally acknowledged in the case of the Lords.

The House of Commons: The first-past-the-post electoral system regularly produces unrepresentative results in the House of Commons. Never since the Second World War has any party won an election and formed a government on the basis of a majority of the votes cast. Conversely, only in nine years since 1945 have governments not enjoyed a working majority. The UK has experienced only one formal coalition government, and this was also the only government that could claim to represent more than 50 per cent of votes cast.

A highly adversarial culture in the Commons is at the root of, and also a consequence of, this electoral system. Especially in recent years, this culture may have played a role in weakening public respect for, and trust in, the legislature (although the British Social Attitudes survey quoted earlier shows that there has never been much readiness to believe that politicians tell the truth 'when in a tight corner'). The theatre of Commons debate – particularly at the weekly Prime Minister's Questions – may make addictive viewing for Westminster aficionados, but its partisan aggressiveness can all too easily alienate or dismay the general public.

The case for this system has always been that it produces stable governments and a strong opposition whose role (as Her Majesty's Most Loyal Opposition) is to hold those governments to account as assertively and aggressively as possible. Its weakness is that it tends to polarise opinion and to inhibit the development of consensus. This in turn makes it more challenging for the executive to plan, invest, and implement for the medium term. Only at times of extreme national crisis have the two major parties come together to form a national unity government, the last being in the Second World War. Not even the pandemic has produced such cooperation across the floor of parliament.

Defenders of the system point to the instability of systems based on proportional representation. Israel is one notorious example, but Italy is the textbook case among our near neighbours. It has had over sixty governments since the Second World War, almost all of them fragile coalitions. Italian politics has suffered from repeated constitutional crises, regional separatism, corruption, and failure to confront long-term strategic economic and societal challenges. As a result, it has for many years been the slowest growing major economy in Europe. Its parliamentary system is part cause and part consequence of the chronic weakness of the Italian state – a weakness whose origins lie deep in Italian history. No analysis of the UK's dilemmas would invoke the Italian parliamentary system as a role model.

Proponents of a move away from the Westminster system point to New Zealand, which successfully shifted in 1996 from a first-past-the-post system to the same form of proportional representation as is now used in Scotland, Wales, and London. But, among our near neighbours, attention focuses increasingly on Germany – arguably a more relevant comparator in size and social complexity, in any case – whose post-war settlement was embodied in a carefully constructed 'basic law' providing for a federal constitution. Germany's settlement was designed from the first to protect the status and interests of the *Länder*, which had been the major units of devolved government under the Allied occupation in the late 1940s. In Germany, federalism is an entrenched principle which cannot be amended even by the constitutional mechanisms provided for amending the basic law, and the federal government is elected by proportional representation with the famous 5 per cent threshold to prevent the proliferation of fringe parties. This system has demonstrated a remarkably robust balance of stability and responsiveness to shifts in electoral mood, as well as a durable balance between regional and national politics. From its establishment in 1949 until 2020, modern Germany has had eight chancellors, while the UK has had sixteen prime ministers over the same period.[5]

The contrast between governance in the UK and Germany is sharp. Of course, the roots of German federalism go far back into the Holy Roman Empire, just as the roots of English centralism go back to the Norman Conquest. As a result, devolution of administration is nowhere near as strongly embedded in the UK (particularly in England), but opinion polls show a clear popular desire for more decentralisation.[6] Yet when it comes to electoral reform in the Commons itself in order to achieve a fairer balance of representation than the first-past-the-post system, the same opinion polling shows that the public is equally divided on this question. What's more, a proposal to elect the Commons on the same system as is used for the devolved assemblies in Scotland, Wales, and London[7] – which would have achieved demonstrably fairer results – was overwhelmingly rejected (on a low turnout of just over 40 per cent) in the referendum of 2011.

Opinion on electoral reform of the House of Commons is not likely to be tested again in the near term; neither of the two main parties has any incentive to do so, unless they were required to allow it as part of the terms of some future coalition government. In consequence, there seems to be little or no room for a change in the voting system, and hence fairer representation in the Commons, for the foreseeable future. However, it is worth noting that polling also shows that younger voters are much more likely to favour change; moreover, the devolved institutions all operate on proportional representation systems, and it seems highly likely that any newly created devolved institutions would do so too. It may be, therefore, that over the longer term the case for some form of proportional representation in the Commons will gain more traction. In the meantime, adversarial politics rather than consensus building is likely to continue to be the order of the day, with all the disadvantages of sloganising, short-termism, and an inability to build cross-party consensus that this binary approach to political debate brings to national decision-making.

The other issue for the Commons is that, with 650

members, it is arguably too large: it is about 13 per cent larger than the French Assemblée nationale (for a country with almost exactly the same population size) and about the same size as the German Bundestag (for a country with a population about 20 per cent larger than the UK). The United States' House of Representatives has 435 members for a population nearly five times as large. Even Italy – the only other European country to have had as large a lower house as the UK – voted last year to reduce its size by a third. By contrast, when the Cameron government proposed to reduce the House of Commons to 600 members, it faced strong rearguard action in parliament, as a result of which this objective has now been dropped.

Finally, it is significant that the experience base of MPs has significantly changed over the past three decades or so: manual workers have been largely replaced by white-collar workers; a decline in the number of teachers has been matched by the growth in the number of business people; the proportion of lawyers is virtually unchanged (although the number of solicitors has increased, offsetting a decline in barristers). The most significant change is the large growth in the number of MPs who have only ever been politicians or their advisers and agents (up from 21 MPs in 1979 to 107 in 2015). Furthermore, half of all Labour MPs and over 30 per cent of all Conservative

MPs have held political roles immediately before being elected.[8] Given that MPs provide the major talent pool for ministers, it is concerning that so many have no – or relatively limited – experience of the world outside politics.

On the other hand, the same period has seen a major and long overdue increase in diversity: a third of members are now female (compared with just 3 per cent in 1979) and 10 per cent are from BAME backgrounds (compared with 1 per cent in 1979). In terms of social background, therefore, the Commons is more representative of the social profile of voters than it has ever been, though there is still much to do.

The House of Lords: With over 800 members and an archaic medley of membership qualifications, the upper house is clearly far too large. It has also become (notwithstanding many excellent individual members) increasingly lacking in perceived legitimacy and overall effectiveness. When people are asked which government institutions work well or badly, the Commons gets a modest, positive response – but the Lords gets a resounding negative response (half of all those polled felt it works badly, while only 30 per cent thought it works well).[9]

Reform of the House of Lords has been a hardy perennial of British politics for at least a century. Before the First World War, its hereditary membership was a bastion of privilege which regularly sought to undermine the programmes of progressive governments. One of its worst and most shameful moments was surely its rejection of Irish Home Rule just before the outbreak of war. Nevertheless, the long journey of reform was under way by then, in particular with limitations on its power to obstruct a sustained majority in the Commons becoming law in 1911. The next two major changes had to wait half a century and more: the creation of life peerages in 1957 and the removal of (most of) the hereditary peers in 1998. These two changes have almost completely changed the profile of the House of Lords. Further limitations on its power to veto legislation have now largely confined its role to that of scrutiny and of testing the will and readiness of the government to mobilise its support in the Commons.

So why the perceived lack of legitimacy and the widespread conviction that further reform is needed? There are two basic reasons: its size, and the appointment process.

The size of the House of Lords has certainly become an embarrassment, including to its own members. Before the bulk of the hereditary peers were removed in 1998, there were 1,210 members. The reform reduced this number by nearly half. In the following decade or more, however, the number increased again – up to almost 800 by around 2012. Since then, it has hovered around this size, as retirements (possible since 2014) have helped offset new appointments. At these levels, it is by far the largest upper house of any democratic polity in the world.

The appointment process, too, has again and again been a source of disquiet, with accusations of cronyism being levelled at prime ministers from some of the earliest appointments in the years after life peerages were introduced in 1958. In fact, there is no clear upward trend in the average annual number of appointments: Wilson, Blair, and Cameron all used the power to recommend peerages extensively, while Thatcher, Brown, and May, for example, all made much less use of it.[10]

The irony is that a house that once represented an aristocratic society and was in tune with a provincial socio-economic mindset has in recent decades shown itself to be much more metropolitan in its sympathies: anti-Brexit, pro-European, and supportive of an extensive welfare state. The backgrounds of peers are very different even from those of twenty years ago. Around 40 per cent have previously worked in representative politics or served as staffers to politicians; business and professional backgrounds represent over 20 per cent. But the House of Lords' image remains poor. Many see it as an outdated, bloated, comfortable London club for retired MPs and for those with a penchant for titles or with vested interests to protect. Polls consistently show large majorities for its reform and sizeable minorities backing outright abolition.[11]

Various schemes of reform have been suggested. In the minds of many is a basic belief that a legislative assembly should have some form of electoral legitimacy, and most proposals have sought both to reduce its numbers and to establish an elected element (or total membership by election), typically on a different franchise from the House of Commons (e.g. regional and/or proportional representation). However, no reliable consensus has been achieved. Since the compromise on hereditary members in 1998 and the establishment of the Supreme Court in 2009 (on which see below), the only notable reform has been the provision for retirement in 2014. An attempt in 2018 to bring down the membership to 600 through a self-denying ordinance on new appointments by prime ministers was honoured in the breach almost immediately. (Even at 600 members, the Lords would still be the second largest upper house – after China – in the world; the French Senate has 348 members, the German Bundesrat 69, and the US Senate 100.)

Other proposals have sought, for example, to reduce its numbers and increase its perceived legitimacy by removing the ninety-two remaining hereditary positions over time and/or by reducing or eliminating the twenty-six positions held by Anglican bishops, or to set term limits and/or a mandatory retiring age.

The main obstacle to reform, apart from inertia, is that the House of Commons is well aware that a more legitimate composition of the House of Lords would be seen as entitling it to more power at the expense of the Commons. (The US pattern of dysfunctional competition between the Senate and the House of Representatives brings its own evident challenges.) However other European countries have found acceptable ways of managing the relationship between two elected chambers, and there is no reason why the UK could not do likewise.

Suggestions have also been mooted that the House of Lords, and perhaps also the House of Commons, should be based outside London, for example in York, to help rebalance the country by moving the political centre of gravity away from London. The main objection to this is that, away from the centre of executive government, the detached house (or houses) would become mere talking shops. The participation and ready availability of ministers and their officials is the lifeblood of the system. This is not (arguably) a problem that can be solved adequately by virtual connectivity. But there is a separate, and perhaps more logical, case for moving the whole capital, with all branches of government, to a centre outside London. This would, of course, involve enormous expense and have much inertia and special pleading to overcome. It is, however, worth noting how many of the world's larger democracies, either through historical happenstance or as a result of specific decisions, have their capital city separate from their main urban commercial hub. Only France among our major Western comparators is like the UK in that the same city serves as both its capital and its primary commercial centre (although Paris is much less economically dominant in France than London is in the UK).

In sum, the Westminster parliament faces major challenges (much like the creaking palace building in which it sits). Its role will have to undergo change and increased democratisation as the inevitable process of devolution and decentralisation unfolds. The Commons may be unlikely to see much fundamental change in the coming years, even though change must surely come in the end, but the House of Lords cries out for reform. The question is whether this is done piecemeal or whether there is a case for a wholly new approach to its role, powers, and composition.

Before returning to this question, however, we must first examine the issues facing executive government and the judiciary.

Executive government

The coronavirus pandemic would have been testing under any circumstances. But it has painfully exposed some operational weaknesses in the UK's executive. These weaknesses are chronic, and they are not fundamentally dependent on which party is in government.

One weakness is long-standing underfunding, which has seriously reduced the resilience of the state. Repeated public expenditure cuts to the funding of central government departments and agencies over the last decade have seriously eroded the ability to plan and implement policy rapidly and effectively across government. The reduced number of permanent officials has weakened the collective memory within departments of what works and what does not. Without the capacity to make contingency plans and maintain capability outside of immediate priority areas, unexpected problems rapidly turn into crises as central government struggles to respond effectively to events.

But, in addition to the need for sufficient financing, there are wider structural problems to address, affecting ministers, civil servants, and special advisers.

Ministers: British government is hampered by an excess of ministers (there are over ninety of them) and by frequent job changes. The size and turnover of the so-called payroll vote is not found among comparable democracies.[12] The force that produces these features is essentially the short-term political convenience of the government. But they produce malign results, encouraging excessive focus on media management, a tendency to micromanage public sector organisations and their professional leadership, and constant changes of priorities which makes policy implementation difficult.[13]

An important indirect cause of this problem is the electoral system. As noted, the first-past-the-post system usually results in governments with a working majority, which therefore do not need to form coalitions. Coalition governments are typically based on highly specific agreements as to which party gets which jobs: prime ministers in such circumstances do not have the leeway to change the team whenever they think it suits their own political priorities. It is noteworthy that our only recent experience of coalition government – from 2010 to 2015 – had much greater stability and ministerial continuity than is typical in the UK.

The central civil service: Whitehall, the central civil service, constitutes about 10 per cent of the total civil service (which is in turn about 10 per cent of the total public sector workforce). A permanent central civil service is essential to effective and honest government. Its role is to be responsive to the priorities of elected governments while also providing the necessary expertise to ensure the continuity and impartiality of government administration. As digitisation revolutionises working practices and service delivery in all parts of the economy and of society, this role for the central civil service is as important as it has ever been.

A culture of public service, and of promotion and appointment on merit, is critical to maintaining a clear separation between the professional requirements of administration and political decision-making. The leadership of the civil service is required to model this separation between politicians and permanent officials, both within government departments and across Whitehall. The shared culture, values, and experience of working together across departments is key to ensuring a coherent policy approach as ministers seek to allocate resources among competing priorities.

The challenge of nurturing this culture is all the more demanding because of both the impact of digitisation and the requirements imposed by decentralisation and devolution. Since the 1970s, Whitehall has sought to disperse more administrative work around the country, and in recent decades the momentum of devolution has made it significantly more complex to cooperate administratively and implement policy cohesively. This makes a shared culture of public service cooperation all the more important as a vital unifying factor in managing the sensitive relationship between Whitehall and the devolved administrations.

Maintaining the core values of public administration while modernising ways of working continues therefore to be a challenge for the central civil service. It also requires acceptance by politicians that the system benefits them by providing the best available policy advice, grounded in what can (and cannot) be made to work within the law and parliamentary propriety and at a high level of technical competence. The civil service for its part needs to ensure that it is open to outside challenge, and that it is sensitive to the concerns of all parts of the country and society.

Effective administration therefore requires the trust of elected politicians and the respect of wider society in order to function. To achieve that trust and respect, the civil service needs to demonstrate transparency in its procedures for assessment and promotion, a focus on learning new skills (perhaps, above all, in digital administration), and an openness to interaction and partnership with a diverse range of innovative bodies and individuals throughout society. Enhanced reporting by officials to parliamentary and other regional and local representative bodies – as entailed by real devolution – is an important element in building this trust, as is the continued direct responsibility of the civil service to the Westminster parliament through scrutiny by the National Audit Office of the effective use of public money.

In recent years, however, this balance has been jeopardised by a number of developments. Some have been imposed by governments in the name of efficiency. Some have been, frankly, political in motivation, and some have been the result of a more general and well-intended desire to open up public sector administration to achieve a flexibility of management modelled on what is perceived as best practice in the private sector.

Between 2010 and 2016, civil service numbers fell by almost 20 per cent, before recovering about half of this decline in the period leading up to Brexit in 2020.[14] The decline led to a serious loss of policy capability across central government and, in turn, to increased outsourcing of policy advice and delivery – often in an unplanned and highly inefficient way. Central Cabinet Office coordination structures have been weakened and departmental strategic planning capability downgraded by pressures to use the more limited policy resources now available within Whitehall on immediate political priorities. This leaves the system dangerously exposed when new challenges arise.

Furthermore, permanent secretaries and other senior leaders have faced growing political interference in their management responsibilities. This pressure, which has provoked some recent high-profile departures, makes it more difficult to provide honest and impartial advice to ministers, especially when this is politically unpopular. 'Speaking truth to power' requires a belief that career prospects will not be harmed by so doing and that ministers will respect the spirit, as well as the letter, of the Ministerial Code.

On the other hand, senior politicians and influential special advisers have often asserted that the permanent civil service is precisely what lies at the heart of the problem with executive government. The argument is often that the system is too cautious, hostile to innovation, and led by a self-perpetuating priesthood of high officials. And it is indeed essential to recognise the value of ensuring at least some recruitment for senior posts from outside the civil service; in fact, officials with external experience are already a significant part of the senior UK civil service – and not just in specialised, technical functions. But any large common endeavour, whether it is public service or a major publicly quoted company, needs to ensure the sustainability of its operating culture and does so mostly by growing its own wood: in this, Whitehall should be no different. It is thus important to strike the right balance between the benefits of outside experience and challenge on the one hand, and the need to preserve a coherent public service delivery across the departments of government on the other. Hence the continued importance of maintaining a core cadre of permanent officials with deep administrative experience, while ensuring that they reflect in their diversity the population they serve.

By the same token, it is also of paramount importance that appointments to government bodies be made on the basis of experience and expertise. Yet the evidence is that such appointments are increasingly made more on considerations of political loyalty. Peter Riddell, the Commissioner for Public Appointments, wrote on 7 October 2020 expressing serious concerns that the balance between appointment on merit and ministerial involvement is now under threat; he also highlighted the growing number of unregulated appointments.[15] If this trend continues, it will undermine the concept of a politically neutral and professional administration in central government. It is also leading to the less efficient direction of public sector agencies, which find it difficult to recruit the right mix of skills at board level due to political interference in the recruitment process.

Some have looked admiringly at the professionalism of the French administration, with its École nationale d'administration (ENA) which supplies the famous *énarques* who have provided so much of the leadership in politics and business as well as government. But this model is itself under pressure to become less elitist and closed, and to allow for more social diversity and innovation in those advancing to positions of economic or political power. In response, the French government has announced a major reform of the ENA, as a result of which it will become a public management school, with the goal of increasing social and geographic diversity within the French administration. Evidently, the lesson that technical competence, while necessary, is no longer sufficient to win public trust has had to be learned in Paris too.

More recently there have been calls in the UK for more 'disrupters' who might apply the skills suitable for a tech start-up or big data management to the process of government. We believe, however, that while these skills can be complementary, they cannot replace the wider framework of accountable administration and measured risk-taking that are required to manage public resources prudently. Politicians tend to be keen on risk-taking in the abstract and yet unwilling to support those who take the risks and who find that even well-researched risks can sometimes go wrong. There is a temptation to seek dramatic new initiatives to announce, too often based on inadequate consultation and preparation and with unrealistic timescales for delivery. Indeed, the pressures of social media and twenty-four-hour news cycles combined with the sharp growth in the number of media advisers within government have often resulted in public announcements being made without proper analysis across government of their implications.

The drive for rapid results also leads to a tendency to centralise decisions on key issues such as technology or procurement. This in turn exposes serious gaps between those deciding and those having to manage the consequences of decisions based on wishful thinking and attractive presentation rather than the rigorous review of the available evidence. These pressures exist in all governmental systems, of course: major public projects have frequently proven hard to manage efficiently in virtually all of our comparator countries. But Germany, for example, is protected by the federal nature of decision-making, which helps provide more time for reflection and medium-term planning (though it also makes the deflection of responsibility easier when something goes wrong); while in France the close connection between the training of many politicians and senior officials through the ENA and other technical *grandes écoles* ensures a shared discipline of approach and respect for expertise.

Special advisers: The UK central government's problems in managing effective decision-making have been complicated in the last two decades by the substantial increase in the number and prominence of special advisers, both in Whitehall departments and in No. 10 Downing Street. In the 1990s, there were fewer than forty such advisers; now there are over 100.[16] Individual advisers have in some cases become high-profile – and controversial – sources of personal support to ministers, in effect taking a range of political decisions with limited or no wider accountability. Some have interfered in the detail of civil service management decisions with serious consequences for the professionalism of procurement, technology, and human resource management.

Special advisers are now a permanent feature of the Whitehall landscape. At their most effective, they play an important role in ensuring that ministerial preferences are fully understood and in assisting civil servants in dealing with politically sensitive issues. But problems remain: the precise status of special advisers, and the mode and extent of their accountability – both within the hierarchy and outside it – is unclear. And experience suggests that they can become a barrier between ministers and civil servants when they should be a pathway. They can also be a plentiful and disruptive source of leaks, making it harder to maintain the appropriate degree of confidentiality during the assessment of policy options across government.

Finally, there has for decades been an uneasy relationship between No. 10 and the departments of Whitehall. Recently, under administrations led by both of the major parties, prime ministers have sought to bolster their influence over government through increased reliance on key special advisers based in No. 10 – with mixed success. At the same time, governmental effectiveness depends in the end on collective cabinet responsibility and cohesiveness, which in turn requires clarity about who has accountability for which decisions, the basis on which they are taken, and the wider parliamentary responsibility for defending them.

There is a choice for the UK about whether, on the one hand, to refresh and recommit to cabinet government with its distribution of formal decision-making and parliamentary accountability between secretaries of state, overseen by the prime minister and coordinated by the Cabinet Office. This model remains the default legal and constitutional position. Alternatively, on the other hand, a more explicitly centralised, quasi-presidential model could be used with executive power and the concomitant parliamentary accountability explicitly placed in No. 10 and the prime minister's personal team. The current reality is an unsatisfactory fudge with decisions made by the prime minister's advisers subject to no rigorous and effective scrutiny, and cabinet ministers often unable to have significant influence on some of the key decisions in their area of public responsibility. We need to bring decision-making within No. 10 and public accountability to parliament closer together.

The judiciary

The British legal system has long been based on the fundamental principle, firmly embodied in the common law, that the judges must carry out the legislative will of parliament. In the classic formulation of the nineteenth-century constitutional theorist A. V. Dicey, 'Parliament may by statute make or unmake any law, including a law that is violative of international law or that alters a principle of the common law. And the courts are obliged to uphold and enforce it.'[17]

Thus, in the continuing absence of a written constitution with provisions to the contrary, the courts cannot set aside or disregard explicit laws made by parliament. However, under a different line of long-standing authorities, the courts can review whether the executive, like any other public or private body, is or is not acting within the law.

Until the last few years, the role of the judiciary, both in developing the common law and in interpreting and enforcing the statute law of parliament, has enjoyed virtually universal acceptance; indeed, it has been a source of some pride as a bulwark of the British democratic order. Moreover, the 2009 reform that created the Supreme Court has been widely (though not universally) seen as an important improvement. Some criticisms of the establishment of the Court are based on the mistaken belief that it was a whim of the government at the time. In fact, it was the delayed culmination of the great reforms of 1873–5 that created the Supreme Court of Judicature.

However, developments in the fields of human rights and judicial review have raised tensions between ministers and the senior judges, and there have even been instances of ministers publicly criticising the judiciary. In February 2013, for example, the then home secretary accused the judges of making the UK more dangerous by ignoring rules aimed at deporting more foreign criminals, commenting that some judges were choosing to ignore parliament's wishes. And when, in November 2016, the *Daily Mail* published a headline describing three senior judges as 'enemies of the people' in response to one of their decisions on Brexit, the then justice secretary (who has a statutory duty to uphold the independence of the judiciary) issued only brief statements which were widely seen as weak and inadequate.

In a free society, there will always be friction between the branches of government, perhaps especially between the executive and the judiciary. But in this respect, alarm bells have been ringing lately. In particular, the present government seems to have formed the view, especially in the light of the decisions in the two *Miller* cases, that the Supreme Court has been intruding improperly into the political sphere.[18]

In *Miller (1)*, the Supreme Court decided by a majority that the UK government could not, by using the royal prerogative alone, leave the EU without the authority of an act of parliament. In *Miller (2)*, the Court decided unanimously that the prerogative power to prorogue parliament was justiciable, and that in the circumstances the government's advice to the Queen to prorogue in September–October 2019 was contrary to constitutional principle and so void.

The fundamental question that the *Miller* cases raised was how far the royal prerogative, exercised on the advice of ministers – which means essentially the executive power of the state – is or ought to be justiciable. (That it *can* be justiciable was settled as long ago as 1610, in the famous *Case of Proclamations*.) The Supreme Court decided in *Miller (2)* that its justiciability extended, at least in these circumstances, to enforcing constitutional principles. This decision confirmed that such principles can be defined and prescribed in law, and that their observance (or otherwise) can therefore be tested and enforced by the courts.

This view was not without controversy, even within the legal world, and it attracted strong political criticism from some voices in both parliament and the government. It is clearly as a result of these decisions that the Conservative Manifesto for the 2019 general election included the following:

> After Brexit we also need to look at the broader aspects of our constitution: the relationship between the Government, Parliament and the courts; the functioning of the Royal Prerogative; the role of the House of Lords; and access to justice for ordinary people. The ability of our security services to defend us against terrorism and organised crime is critical. We will update the Human Rights Act and administrative law to ensure that there is a proper balance between the rights of individuals, our vital national security and effective government. We will ensure that judicial review is available to protect the rights of individuals against an overbearing state, while ensuring that it is not abused to conduct politics by another means or to create needless delays. In our first years we will set up a Constitution, Democracy and Rights Commission that will examine these issues in depth, and come up with proposals to restore trust in our institutions and in how our democracy operates.[19]

The government has not so far set up such a wide-ranging commission. However, in July 2020, it established an independent review of administrative law, chaired by Lord Faulks QC, to 'consider whether [in the law of judicial review] the right balance is being struck between the rights of citizens to challenge executive decisions and the need for effective and efficient government'. Further, in December 2020, it set up an independent review of the 1998 Human Rights Act, chaired by Sir Peter Gross (a former judge of the Court of Appeal), to examine its workings. At the time of writing, these reviews have not yet reported, so it remains to be seen how far they may propose limitations on the power of the judicial branch of government to uphold the rule of law.

Since the 1960s, judicial review has grown and developed, as its equivalents have in other Western democracies, as a means of keeping governments, both central and local, within constraints of proper procedure and rationality. On the whole, judges in the UK have been careful to respect the proper preserve of ministers. Not surprisingly, however, this has sometimes led to ministerial resentment. A proposal to restrict the general scope of judicial review might be convenient for any government tempted to extend executive power, but it would risk fundamentally undermining the rule of law; it would tip the balance of the UK's constitution away from not only the judiciary but, in effect, also from parliament, in a field where the courts typically act as allies of the latter.

Continuing tensions may well also focus more attention on the way in which senior judges are appointed. Indeed, they will almost certainly do so if it is accepted (as we argue in Part 2) that the UK should move towards a more codified constitutional settlement. Such a settlement would be highly likely to (and should) have at least some entrenched clauses, which almost certainly would (and should) in turn be interpreted by the Supreme Court. The Supreme Court would therefore in effect be empowered to review parliamentary legislation that contravenes those clauses.

That in turn would draw more attention to the background and views of the judges, as well as to who appoints them and how. The current system of appointing Supreme Court judges, under which a committee of senior judges and selected lay members presents the Lord Chancellor with a single nomination, has so far worked reasonably well – though there are concerns about diversity and self-perpetuation. But in our view, the judges will need strengthening against further and possibly more damaging political attack. The main obstacle here, apart from inertia, is the strong and understandable opposition of the judicial and legal community to any involvement of politicians in the system. We return to this point in Part 2, with some specific proposals for reform.

A crisis with many facets

A former Archbishop of York once described the British constitution as being like a ball of wool: once you start pulling at its threads, you never know where it will stop – and you certainly won't be able to ravel it up again.[20] The ball of wool is now unravelling, with potentially existential consequences for the United Kingdom. The habits and understandings – the unwritten rules – which have been at the basis of this country's governance for centuries are being put to the gravest test since the birth of the Union. The crisis affects all branches of government: legislature, executive, and judiciary. We believe that what is now required is not another ad hoc response of the kind we have seen at various points in the history of the Union. What the country needs is nothing less than a new constitutional settlement. We will now set out proposals for such a settlement.

Part 2: A New Constitutional Settlement

In proposing a way forward in the face of the UK's crisis of governance, we believe that a new constitutional settlement is both necessary and inevitable. Such a settlement must have as its fundamental principle a federal approach that accommodates devolution and decentralisation – not just as awkward facts of modern life but as the best way of facilitating a successful and diverse national life in the coming century. And it must be systematic, not another ad hoc patchwork.

This part makes specific proposals for such a constitutional settlement. We intend it as a contribution to what we feel is inevitably going to become an increasingly topical national debate. In making our proposals, we assume that under any scenario there will continue to be:

- A United Kingdom, consisting of England and one or more of Wales, Scotland, and Northern Ireland
- A constitutional monarchy with the same

limits to its formal authority as at present

- Legislative sovereignty of parliament (except as modified by entrenched clauses of any future codified constitution)
- An executive drawn from, and answerable to, the legislature
- A non-partisan, permanent civil service, recruited and promoted on merit
- An independent, non-political judiciary appointed and promoted on merit, whose senior members enjoy the security of tenure granted by the Act of Settlement 1701
- A human rights regime, whether under the European Convention on Human Rights or an equivalent British replacement.

None of these principles is likely to be called into question by any but a tiny minority of the public in general or of politicians in particular. But there is one further assumption we make that would be contested by a more significant minority of commentators: we argue for a bicameral legislature (as is commonly – but not universally – the case in other comparable democratic systems). We argue this partly on the basis that throughout the whole history of the British state the legislature has been bicameral, but also importantly on the basis that a radically reformed upper house would play an essential role in a new, more federal UK constitution.

So what form should the new, federal UK system of governance take? The answer is shaped by the need to address two issues: one arises from the sheer size of England in relation to the whole of the UK; the other from the long-standing constitutional principle that the legislative will of parliament is sovereign.

Resolving the English problem

No system that keeps England as a bloc on its own could work: the disparity of its size with the other nations is simply too great. Furthermore, diversity within England itself is arguably growing: between urban and rural areas, former industrial regions and service centres, London and the rest of the country. The creation of an English parliament notionally parallel to the legislatures of the other three nations would therefore cause more problems than it would solve. Accordingly, any version of federalism for the UK must include splitting up England into separate areas or units. For the reasons set out in Part 1, there are currently no historically rooted identities that can readily serve as the basis for the federalisation of England. But there are compelling reasons for decentralisation in the name of greater efficiency and responsiveness of public service, and we believe that if it is to be sustainable, this has to be accompanied by properly empowered and accountable democratic representation.

The answer to this dilemma must therefore be an explicit strategy to build on the progress already made in the past decade through the establishment of directly elected metropolitan mayoralties. These should become the backbone of the emerging political decentralisation of England. The eleven urban areas with populations of more than half a million represent 42 per cent of the total population of England;[21] the total of all urban areas represents over 80 per cent of the population.[22] Directly elected mayoralties covering all these urban areas would thus transform English public life by dramatically increasing public engagement with, and power to decide on, regional and local issues.

That localised power must include the revival of a local tax base separate from Westminster control. This separation would allow for partnership funding between local, regional, and national authorities for infrastructure, social housing, transport, and other projects determined by democratic decision-making. Such partnership funding is regularly used in other European countries and indeed internationally. Poorer areas would still receive more support from central government, and health and social security would remain nationally funded (consistent with the deep-rooted national belief that health and welfare are rights that all should enjoy). But the level of local property and business tax receipts and how they are spent would reflect local democratic decisions for which directly elected local mayors and other local politicians would be accountable.

This approach would require a new partnership between central and devolved governments recognising separate and shared areas of responsibility, and a conscious rejection both of the automatic equivalence of all local service levels and of central treasury micromanagement of local spending. Other countries manage the compromise and mutual respect involved between different levels of government; so can we.

The question remains of what to do about the democratic empowerment of the more rural parts of the country. It may be appropriate that their involvement in the newer, federal approach would be voluntary and gradual, possibly based on existing county structures. This outcome would imply a continuation, maybe for some time, of a pattern in which the new exists alongside the old. But the vast majority of the population would live in areas covered by the new devolved approach.

Moving to a federal constitution

There can be no effective federalism without two major changes to the way the UK is governed: first, effective federalism would require what amounts to a codified constitution, at least for the purpose of establishing the federation; second, it entails reform of the parliamentary system. This section sets out the case for each of these two changes.

A codified constitution: This is entailed by a federal system that distributes power away from the centre. The UK has already started on this journey, and it is irreversible. While it may theoretically be the case that a single act of the Westminster parliament could entirely revoke the devolution settlements with Scotland, Wales, and Northern Ireland, this is plainly unrealistic. The UK government has recently shown a desire to rein in devolved government, but the risk that this would simply encourage the centrifugal tendencies in the nations of the Union is obvious. Moreover, as England necessarily moves along the road towards decentralisation, as argued earlier, the powers of directly elected mayoralties will have to be extended and embodied in legislation that would surely also become, in reality if not in theory, irrevocable. All in all, such devolving legislation will increasingly be tantamount to a new, codified constitutional settlement.

The UK is alone among developed countries in not having a written codified constitution (Israel has no single basic law or formal constitution either, but it does have a series of basic laws, some of which can only be changed by a supermajority in the Knesset). The reasons for this are of course historical, notably including the fact that, unlike the Americans and the French, the UK has had no revolution since the Union was formed in 1707, nor has it had a moment of total political collapse followed by a completely new start requiring a new constitution, as in the case of Germany, Italy, and France in the aftermath of the Second World War.

The evolution of the British system has, in fact, been famously ad hoc. Some would celebrate a continuity extending all the way back to the Magna Carta eight centuries ago – though to do so is arguably to overlook or downplay both the role of the common law and also some sharp disjuncts in British constitutional history. But it is part of the British self-understanding today that parliament alone makes laws and can amend or repeal any existing law if it so chooses. Moreover, the British political culture has always exalted 'flexibility' and the corresponding benefits of pragmatism over 'legalism'. This pragmatism has in turn been underpinned to some extent by the continuity and political neutrality of the civil service and by the growth of judicial review (both now under threat, as argued in Part 1); it has also been underpinned by a shared political culture (which is now eroding).

These reasons underlying the UK's unwritten constitution have had historical relevance, but the now inevitable requirement for significant further decentralisation demands radical change. The UK system has always provided for elected representation at local authority level. What is new is major devolution – to the three smaller nations of the UK and, increasingly, to directly elected metropolitan mayors in England, whose powers, including tax and borrowing powers, will grow.

Against this background, the case for a new and codified constitutional settlement has grown steadily stronger in recent years. The obstacles are formidable, certainly: for one thing, the empirical pragmatism and traditionalism of English attitudes militate against major systemic changes, especially if they are perceived to be complex or imposed by fiat and if they don't fit all specific circumstances neatly. (Thus, for example, the Cameron government's effort to reduce the size of the Commons to 600 broadly equal constituencies was partly bedevilled by the 'Isle of Wight question'.) But we believe that there is now no alternative but to confront those obstacles. The significance of the change entailed by devolution is becoming ever clearer.

It is an inescapable implication that a new codified constitutional settlement will entail giving the Supreme Court the power to interpret it, and to set aside legislative actions of parliament that it holds to be in contravention of the constitution. Moreover, there would almost certainly have to be at least some entrenched clauses, especially about the process for constitutional amendments and probably about human rights. Such entrenched clauses could only be amended either by a plebiscite under specific and controlled procedures or – more likely and more appropriately, perhaps – by a supermajority of, say, two-thirds in parliament. Both of these aspects would be viewed with suspicion by some, in the House of Commons in particular, as diminutions of parliamentary sovereignty. It would also be argued that this would give further impetus to the inevitable 'legalisation', not only of British constitutional development but of government in general. At a time when the involvement of the judges in governmental issues has become seen in some quarters as 'political', codification is unlikely to be popular with many professional politicians.

Despite these objections, however, Westminster and Whitehall will now surely find themselves being pushed down this path. In reality, the choice is between a proactive strategy to embrace the consequences of devolution and an ultimately unsuccessful rearguard action against it, because a body of law is already emerging, the core of which increasingly looks irrevocable in practice. Parliamentary sovereignty is not untrammelled in the way that some purists proclaim. Besides, it is an English doctrine only, and one that Scotland has explicitly never fully accepted – a significant divergence which will become relevant in the forthcoming tussle between Holyrood and Westminster.[23] In our view, it would therefore be better to be proactive in advancing on this journey, rather than being forced (by Scotland or by the major metropolitan mayors of England) to react to the build-up of pressure.

This new constitutional settlement will require an act of parliament, which would in effect be a 'basic law', analogous to the basic law that embodies the German constitution. Some traditionalists might hold that parliament cannot legislate away its own sovereignty in this way; we believe, on the contrary, that the legal and political realities now point in a different direction, reflecting the irreversible changes that have occurred and are continuing within the UK, and which require a matching response in our democratic representation.

Reform of the parliamentary system: While we think that the case for reforming the House of Commons is strong, we accept that the impetus for it has run out of steam in recent years. Without taking it off the agenda, therefore, for the time being we assume no major change in the size, composition, or electoral basis of the Commons (other than the changes that would be brought about by a vote for Scottish independence).

The state of the House of Lords, on the other hand, cries out for urgent reform. A historic opportunity therefore presents itself: to reposition the Lords as, in effect, the federal upper house and to reshape it in a way that represents the interests of a radically decentralised UK. Its fundamental purpose would be to embody and uphold the new constitutional settlement, and this purpose would define its powers.

This new upper house would become an entirely elected body, with the associated democratic legitimacy that this confers, and its electoral basis would be deliberately differentiated from the simple first-past-the-post system of the Commons, thereby providing some balance to the inbuilt bias towards a binary adversarial structure in the lower house. We argue that the electoral basis of the reformed upper house should be the same proportional representation system as is used for Scotland, Wales, and London: the so-called 'additional member' system. Around a quarter of the population lives in areas where this system is already used in devolved parliament/assembly elections, and is familiar with it.

Within Westminster, we believe that the House of Commons should retain primacy with regard to taxation and spending, as is the case in most comparator bicameral systems (with the US as the only major – and highly dysfunctional – exception). Hence the reformed

House of Lords would – as at present – have no power to vote and decide on money bills.[24] Following from this, we argue for the continuation of the present convention (or at least understanding) that the prime minister should be a member of the House of Commons. Conversely, and as a consequence of the fundamental role of the reformed House of Lords in upholding the constitutional settlement, we argue that it should have the right to veto any proposed legislation that amends or impacts that settlement. The Parliament Act would therefore need to be amended to reflect this new veto power.

We also contend that electoral terms in the upper house should be different from – and longer than – those in the Commons. One option would be non-renewable terms of ten or fifteen years; another would be eight-year terms that are renewable (subject to re-election) once. Such longer terms should enable members to develop expertise and experience in the discharge of their responsibilities; it would also create something of a sheet anchor in the swirling currents of political debate in the Commons.

Elections would take place on a fixed cycle. One option would be to elect a third of the upper house every five years; another would, if on eight-year terms, be to elect half of the house every four years. Whichever option is chosen, the cycle would not alter to reflect any out-of-cycle Commons elections that might be called. The consequence of this decision would be that, although the government of the day could still ask the Sovereign to dissolve parliament in order to seek a new mandate and a working majority in the Commons, it could not be assured of a working majority in the upper house (which is in fact the position all governments have found themselves in since the removal of hereditary peers in 1998).

Other important questions would need to be addressed and would also require appropriate revisions. For instance, should any members be indirectly elected (as in the case of the German Bundesrat)? If so, how? Should the system build in special provision for representation by social groups that would otherwise risk being marginalised? For example, a weighting could give a stronger voice to rural views in an otherwise heavily urban society (each county could elect representatives, but all counties could have at least a minimum number regardless of population). And should the ex officio representation of Anglican bishops continue (we assume not)?

There is a case for a separate, smaller national body, with advisory responsibilities but no legislative power, which might include people with the sort of profile currently represented on the crossbenches of the House of Lords, including a range of religious and other community leaders. Indeed, this role could be given to a renewed Privy Council, giving it the right to be consulted and to comment on significant economic and social issues deserving wider national debate. However, this possibility should be considered only as an adjunct to the reform of the upper house we have proposed: we do not in any way see it as an alternative option.

Strengthening executive capacity

In addition to a new constitutional settlement, we also believe that significant new measures are necessary to ensure the robustness of executive government. Specifically, we believe that efficiency and effectiveness require: a new approach to departments and ministerial portfolio allocation; a reinvestment in the capacities of the civil service; and clarification of the role of special advisers.

Ministerial portfolios: The number of ministers should be substantially reduced, and ministers should not be moved as frequently as at present. As noted above, the Westminster government has more ministers than any comparable country, plus an increasing number of special advisers to support them. To achieve more transparent and effective government, the number of ministers should be limited to no more than four in any single department, with clearer powers and responsibilities set out for each role. Apart from exceptional circumstances requiring early dismissal, no minister at any level should serve fewer than about thirty months in their post, and preferably three years or more.

Departmental boundary changes should remain an option for government, but such changes should require prior discussion and agreement in parliament and, where appropriate, across all the UK nations. This will avoid the damaging disruption caused by unexpected changes in departmental responsibilities which add to the costs and difficulty of service delivery and can reduce efficiency for a number of years.

The central civil service: To balance legitimate ministerial priorities while continually modernising delivery methods, we need a confident and properly resourced civil service. This requires strategic career planning and high-quality training in management, as well as specific departmental expertise.

Traditionally, career planning for senior leaders in the civil service has involved working in several departments and often a posting to the centre of government in the Cabinet Office to understand how government as a whole is best coordinated and led as a single structure. Promotion needs to take account of relevant experience accumulated in this way, alongside core management and leadership skills. It has to be seen to be independent of political influence to ensure that ambitious officials do not tell ministers what they would like to hear as a route to promotion.

Equally, the promotion process needs to involve outside expertise to ensure that senior civil servants are competent in managing the challenges of modern administration, reflect the diversity of UK society, and compare well with the best leaders of the private and third sectors. External appointments help prevent a culture of 'inbreeding' within Whitehall, but such appointments need to be made rigorously to ensure both that public sector values are maintained and that there is no overt or implicit political pressure involved in appointment decisions. To do so, government needs to reaffirm the role of public appointment bodies by giving them increased powers over all such appointments in order to counteract the recent erosion of their influence; increased parliamentary scrutiny is also needed to ensure the correct procedures have been followed. Finally, government decisions to override the recommendations of public appointment bodies should be subject to potential judicial review in the case of senior appointments.

The ability of civil servants to train each other, as well as to draw on external sources, is key to maintaining the collective culture of government so policy can be developed and delivered on the basis of shared values. The abolition of the National School of Government (formerly the Civil Service College) in 2012 was a serious error, and the school urgently needs to be revived to provide a forum for the systematic sharing of experience – about what works well and lessons learned from what goes wrong. In an era when there is inevitably more movement in and out of the public sector in general, and of the central civil service in particular, this is more important than ever.

Special advisers: These posts should not be allowed to function as a separate layer of government. It is important that civil service advice is sent directly to ministers, with comments from advisers but without their being able to censor or even stop the advice from reaching ministers. Ministers remain responsible for political and policy decisions, and they need to have seen relevant professional and impartial advice if they are to be effective in the responsibilities for which they are accountable to parliament. Special advisers should also be required to respect the confidence of cross-governmental discussion without seeking to use the media to present their own ministers in the most favourable light.

No. 10 and governmental departments: It is notoriously difficult to get the balance right between No. 10 and departments and, within that balance, the roles of ministers, special advisers and officials. However, governmental success depends on doing so. In the end, this is a matter of wisdom in the choice of appointments and the prime minister's management of the cabinet. But we believe it is now critically important to clarify and codify how a cohesively run government structure is to function consistently with existing parliamentary scrutiny and civil service neutrality.

The balance between executive power and responsibility to parliament has been seriously disturbed by the trend in recent decades for No. 10 to intervene ever more extensively in the detail of departmental policy making and operations. Whatever level of central power a prime minister decides to exercise, it needs to be made transparent and subject to much better scrutiny. So, for instance, if there is to be continued centralisation of power within the prime minister's office, this power must be clearly delineated and subject to greater parliamentary accountability; the lead No. 10 adviser could, for example, appear together with the relevant departmental minister before committees to answer questions and respond to reports.

Maintaining an independent judiciary

The role of the judiciary in the governance of the UK is now more important than ever, in spite of recent government initiatives to limit it. There is no choice about this: devolution makes it inevitable, and the more devolution grows, the more judicial involvement will do so too.

We therefore strongly advise against any general restrictions on the scope of judicial review, or generally the role of the courts as a branch of government. To do so could seriously endanger the rule of law. Indeed, the reforms of the wider constitution that we propose would – and should – give the courts a wider, not a narrower, role than at present. Equally strongly, we recommend that ministers punctiliously obey their duty not to make public criticisms of individual judges and judicial decisions or of the judiciary in general. They should also have the courage to defend it when under ideological attack from parliamentarians or from sections of the media.

One way of buttressing the senior judges against further political attack – which the reforms we propose are likely to bring in their wake – would be to restore to the process of appointing them a carefully delineated element of participation by the other branches of government. As mentioned above, the legal and judicial communities are widely opposed to any involvement of elected politicians in the appointments system. However, these communities arguably do not yet perceive either the full implications (in this context) of the fact that the judiciary are one of three branches of government, or the dangers that seem increasingly likely to threaten them. We believe, on the contrary, that the senior judiciary will increasingly need the confirmation and protection that some involvement of the executive and legislative participation in their appointment could bring. Such involvement will need careful and detailed formulation, which should include proper safeguards to ensure that selection continues to be on merit and without political partiality.

We propose that this should be achieved by two changes to the existing process of appointment in the case of Supreme Court judges. First, the Judicial Appointments Commission should present the Lord Chancellor with two candidates, as happens in other cases where government is involved in senior public (and ecclesiastical) appointments. It would then be for the Lord Chancellor to recommend one of them to the Sovereign. Second, a judiciary committee of the reformed and elected upper house should hold an annual hearing both with the Judicial Appointments Commission and with the president of the Supreme Court, and ad hoc hearings with newly appointed members of the Court.

Of course, the risk of restoring such 'political' involvement in judicial appointments is of the slippery slope towards a US-style politicisation on party lines. The countervailing risk in not doing so is of leaving judges isolated and defenceless against parliamentary, as well as executive, hostility when they make decisions that the political class regards as beyond their province – and we have already seen some of this. (Even the judges' individual security of tenure under the Act of Settlement 1701 will not suffice for this purpose, since what is at stake is not just individual independence from political pressure but that of the judicial branch of government as a whole.)

It will be necessary to find the right balance, certainly, but these issues will not go away as the UK moves (as we think is inevitable) towards a codified constitutional settlement. And getting it right is crucial to upholding the rival claims of elective democracy and the rule of law.

It is perhaps unnecessary to state that we also advise strongly against suggestions from some quarters in Westminster to downgrade the Supreme Court, either by returning it to its former position as a committee of the House of Lords or otherwise. It is the highest, indeed the only, mainstream court in the UK, and it has – and will have – a key role in regulating present and future arrangements for devolution across the UK and within England.

The way forward

These proposals are only the bare outlines of a radical reform of our governmental institutions; many important elements of course remain to be filled in. But in their essence, the main conclusions form an interconnected programme and should, in our judgement, be considered and implemented together. In summary, our central proposals are that:

- The United Kingdom should now move decisively towards a federal system of government.
- The new federal system should be the framework for a major devolution of powers and functions to the four nations, amounting to 'home rule'.
- Democratic devolution should be extended to all the urban areas of England.
- The new federal framework and governmental system should be embodied in a codified written constitution or 'basic law' contained in an act of parliament.
- This constitution should include entrenched clauses, especially and at least concerning its own amendment, and it should be interpreted by the Supreme Court of the United Kingdom.
- The House of Lords should be transformed into a democratic federal upper house, much smaller than at present, directly elected on the additional member system, and representing the nations and regions.
- The reformed House of Lords should have a

veto on any proposed legislation that would amend or impact the constitution or its working.

- However, the House of Commons should continue to have a monopoly on taxation and spending (except the portion that is devolved to the nations and regions).
- The House of Commons should also be reformed in its numbers, mode of election, and culture. However, this can await a later stage, perhaps depending on the effect on the parliamentary system of the reform of the House of Lords.

It is worth stressing that if Scotland does become independent, we still advocate these reforms for the remaining nations of the United Kingdom.

Initiating such a programme of reforms will clearly be a major task, and it calls for discussion far beyond the usual political and academic circles. But major political players need to be willing to take up the cause. The best case for doing so – urgently – is surely that it offers the most promising way both to improve the quality of government across the whole of the UK and to persuade the nations (especially Scotland) of the advantages of staying in the Union.

The UK government must of course take the lead in this, though a degree of cross-party agreement would be essential. But that can only be the beginning: we believe there needs to be a constitutional commission, convened by royal command at the request of government in parliament, with suitably diverse membership and an effective supporting team. Its aim would be to engage with a range of groups across the country on how we can increase democratic control over local and national decision-making, protect judicial independence, and modernise our national political structures.

This commission would have the multiple tasks of steering the project, organising the national discussion, reaching conclusions, and presenting them to parliament and the public. At every stage of this process, each of the four nations would need to be closely involved, and the results would need to command the broad and continuing support of all their national representative assemblies. Last but not least, the UK government would need to have the will and perseverance to carry all this into effect. This may take some – but hopefully not too many – years. Nevertheless, it is vital to begin the national discussion now. The true glory will be in continuing the task to the end.

Acknowledgements

We would especially like to thank John Llewellyn, Andrew Gowers, Jeremy Greenstock, Nick Greenstock, Gerald Holtham, and Alexis Lautenberg – all of the Policy Reform Group – for their helpful and insightful comments on the paper which we wrote for the PRG and which formed the basis for this book. We also want to thank Harry Hall, Alice Horne and the team at Haus Publishing for the remarkable efficiency and speed with which they helped us in bringing it to fruition. All have been a delight to work with, and all have helped significantly to improve our work – though of course we take full responsibility for the outcome.

Notes

1   See, for example, *The Times*'s 2021 State of the Union/YouGov poll, which puts support for independence at 23 per cent. Tim Shipman and Jason Allardyce, 'Union in crisis as polls reveal voters want referendum on Scottish independence and united Ireland', *The Times* (Jan. 2021), accessed online.

2   John Curtice, Nathan Hudson, and Ian Montagu, eds, *British Social Attitudes: The 37th Report*. London: The National Centre for Social Research, 2020.

3   'Global Credit Research', Moody's Investors Service Paris (2020), accessed online.

4   The decentralisation of financial power is not without risk, but it is important not to draw the wrong lessons from episodes in which local authorities have acted *ultra vires* or incompetently in investing funds borrowed from the Treasury. The right course is to ensure responsible administration

through transparency and accountability, for which direct election is essential.

5   See John Kampfner's *Why the Germans do it Better* (London, 2020), with its provocative subtitle 'Notes from a Grown-up Country', for a sophisticated and nuanced analysis of the strengths and weaknesses of a country which has sustained a strong economy and a well-resourced and well-managed welfare system, as well as surmounting the enormous challenge of reunification. Its performance during the pandemic has been indisputably the best of all the major countries of Europe.

6   'The YouGov Democracy Study', YouGov, 2020, accessed online.

7   Under the so-called additional member system (sometimes called the mixed member proportional system), each voter casts two votes: one for a candidate standing for their own constituency, as in the first-past-the-post system, and one for a party list covering a wider area made up of multiple constituencies. The result makes the overall election result more proportional to votes cast than the existing Westminster system.

8   'Social Background of MPs 1979–2019', House of Commons Briefing Paper 7483, 2020.

9   'The YouGov Democracy Study', op. cit.

10 David Beamish, 'United Kingdom Peerage Creations 1801 to 2019', www.peerages.info (2020), accessed online.

11 See 'Poll: Support for House of Lords at 'rock bottom' as public overwhelmingly back overhaul', Electoral Reform Society (Sept. 2020) accessed online.

12 Peter Riddell, 'British Government is hampered by an excess of ministers and frequent job changes', *Prospect* (2019), accessed 27 Jan. 2020.

13 Peter Riddell, *15 Minutes of Power: The Uncertain Life of British Ministers* (London, 2019).

14 See 'Civil service staff numbers', Institute of Government (Jan. 2021), accessed online.

15 'Letter from the Commissioner for Public Appointments to Lord Evans [the Chair of the Committee on Standards in Public Life]', gov.uk (Nov. 2020).

16 See 'Annual Report on Special Advisers 2020', Cabinet Office (Dec. 2020), accessed online.

17 A. V. Dicey, *The Law of the Constitution* (1885), pp.39–40.

18 *R. (ex p. Miller) v. Secretary of State for Exiting the EU* [2017] UKSC 5; *R. (ex p. Miller) v. The Prime*

Minister; Cherry et al. v. Advocate General for Scotland [2019] UKSC 41.

19 'Get Brexit Done; Unleash Britain's Potential: The Conservative and Unionist Party Manifesto 2019', *Conservative Party* (2019), p.48.

20 Reported private communication. The Rt Reverend the Lord Habgood, Archbishop of York 1983–1995, was known for his deep engagement with the role of the Church of England in the life of the nation.

21 These major conurbations are: Greater London, Greater Manchester, West Midlands, West Yorkshire, Liverpool, South Hampshire, Tyneside, Nottingham, Sheffield, Bristol and Leicester.

22 Essentially, all built up areas with at least 10,000 inhabitants, as defined by the Office for National Statistics.

23 *MacCormick* v. *Lord Advocate* (1953) SC 396, in which Lord President Cooper observed that 'the principle of the unlimited sovereignty of Parliament is a distinctively English principle which has no counterpart in Scottish constitutional law'. See also the Scottish government's announcement on 19 December 2020 that 'Parliamentary sovereignty is no longer an accurate description of the constitution in

Scotland or the UK', *Scottish Legal News* (Dec. 2019), accessed online.

24 Money bills are those which, in the opinion of the Speaker of the House of Commons, are concerned only with national taxation, public money, or loans.

HAUS CURIOSITIES

Inspired by the topical pamphlets of the interwar years, as well as by Einstein's advice to 'never lose a holy curiosity', the series presents short works of opinion and analysis by notable figures. Under the guidance of the series editor, Peter Hennessy, Haus Curiosities have been published since 2014.

Welcoming contributions from a diverse pool of authors, the series aims to reinstate the concise and incisive booklet as a powerful strand of politico-literary life, amplifying the voices of those who have something urgent to say about a topical theme.

Britain in a Perilous World: The Strategic Defence and Security Review We Need
JONATHAN SHAW

The UK's In-Out Referendum: EU Foreign and Defence Policy Reform
DAVID OWEN

Establishment and Meritocracy
PETER HENNESSY

Greed: From Gordon Gekko to David Hume
STEWART SUTHERLAND

The Kingdom to Come: Thoughts on the Union Before and After the Scottish Referendum
PETER HENNESSY

Art, Imagination and Public Service
DAVID BLUNKETT, MICHEAL O'SIADHAIL, BRENDA
HALE, HUGHIE O'DONOGHUE, CLARE MORIARTY AND
JAMES O'DONNELL

Justice in Public Life
CLAIRE FOSTER-GILBERT, JAMES HAWKEY AND
JANE SINCLAIR

The London Problem: What Britain Gets Wrong About Its Capital City
JACK BROWN